WEATHER AROUND YOU

ANGELA ROYSTON

WAYLAND

GEOGRAPHY STARTS HERE!

Weather Around You

OTHER TITLES IN THE SERIES
Hills and Mountains · Maps and Symbols
Rivers and Streams · Where People Live
Your Environment

Produced for Wayland Publishers Limited by
Lionheart Books
10, Chelmsford Square
London NW10 3AR
England

Designer: Ben White

Editor: Lionel Bender

Picture Research: Madeleine Samuel

Electronic make-up: Mike Pilley, Radius.

Illustrated by Rudi Visi and Peter Bull

First Published in 1997 by Wayland Publishers Limited
61 Western Road, Hove, East Sussex BN3 1JD
© Copyright 1997 Wayland Publishers Limited

Find Wayland on the internet at http://www.wayland.co.uk

British Library Cataloguing in Publication Data
Royston, Angela
Weather around you. – (Geography starts here!)
1. Weather – Juvenile literature
I. Title II. Bender, Lionel
551.6

ISBN 0 7502 1991 2

Printed and bound by L.E.G.O. S.p.A., Vicenza, Italy

Picture Acknowledgements:
Pages 1: Lionheart Books. 4: Zefa. 5, 6-7: Zefa/Stockmarket. 8: Skjold/Wayland Publishers Limited.
11: Eye Ubiquitous/T. Nottingham. 12: Wayland Publishers Limited. 13: Zefa. 14: Eye
Ubiquitous/NASA. 15: Zefa/N. Y. Gold. 16-17 top: Zefa/Flury. 16-17 bottom:
Zefa/Stockmarket/D. Durance 11. 19: Wayland Publishers Limited. 20: James Davis Travel
Photography. 21: Eye Ubiquitous/A. J. G. Bell. 22: Zefa. 23: Wayland Publishers. 24: Frank Lane
Photo Library/D. Hoadley. 25: Zefa/Henley and Savage. 26, 27: Zefa. 28: Wayland Publishers
Limited. 29: Zefa/Stockmarket. 29: Zefa. 30: Wayland Publishers Limited. Cover: Zefa.

The photo on the previous page shows a beach scene on a hot but windy day at Cape Cod, USA.

CONTENTS

WHAT IS WEATHER?

What is the weather like today? Is it hot, sunny, cold or windy? In some places it may be dry one day, and rainy the next. In other places, it may be hot and dry, or freezing cold for weeks on end.

The weather affects the clothes we wear, the houses we live in and the food we eat. It also affects when and where we go on holiday.

These people in New York, USA, have decided to take a taxi to get out of the rain.

4

This woodland in Oregon, USA, is filled with orange leaves on a bright day in autumn.

TEMPERATURE

The Sun heats the land and sea, and they heat the air above them. Temperature tells us how hot or cold somewhere is.

Countries near the Equator (an imaginary line around the middle of the Earth) get the strongest sunshine and so they are the hottest. The further away from the Equator a place is, the weaker the sunshine and the cooler the air.

The Rocky Mountains in Wyoming, USA, are often covered by snow in winter.

SUNSHINE

See for yourself why sunshine is strongest at the Equator, using a ball and a torch.

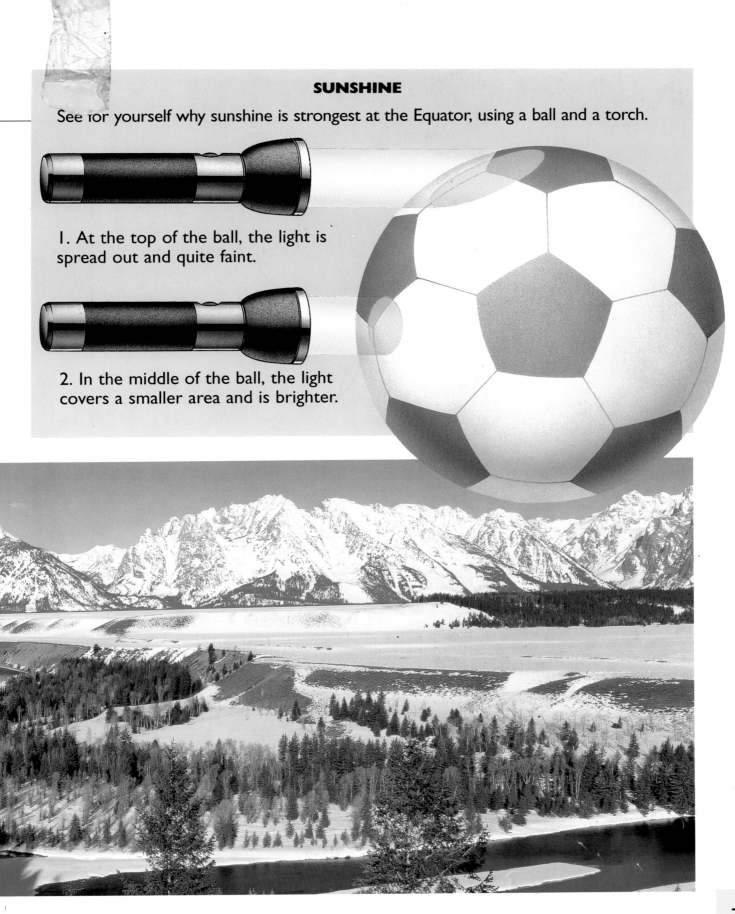

1. At the top of the ball, the light is spread out and quite faint.

2. In the middle of the ball, the light covers a smaller area and is brighter.

Playing in snow can be lots of fun. But it is important to wear warm clothes.

Hot and Cold

Either side of the Equator lie the tropical regions of the Earth. Tropical regions have mainly hot, damp weather almost all year round.

Temperate regions, such as much of Europe and North America, have mild weather all year round. Areas near the North and South Poles are freezing cold for most of the year.

MEASURING TEMPERATURE

Find out the coldest place in and around your home. Using a room thermometer, measure the temperature of the following places:

1 In the middle of a room.

2 On a sunny window ledge.

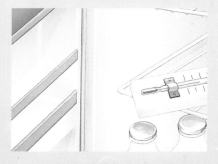

3 In the refrigerator.

4 Outside in the shade.

The Four Seasons

The Earth takes one year to move around the Sun. As it does so, the temperature in different parts of the world changes. These changes create the four main seasons – spring, summer, autumn and winter.

The Earth is slightly tilted. As the Earth moves around the Sun, the seasons change north and south of the Equator.

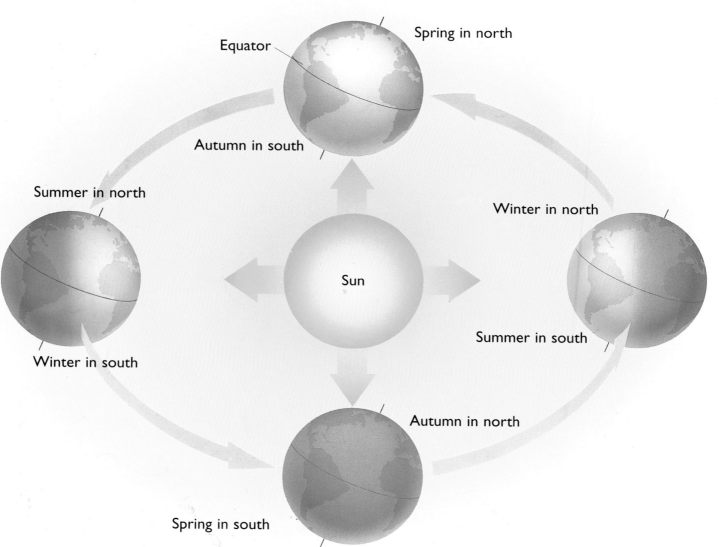

Equator

Spring in north

Autumn in south

Summer in north

Winter in south

Sun

Winter in north

Summer in south

Autumn in north

Spring in south

In spring, plants begin to grow and many animals give birth to young. Summer is the hottest season. In autumn, plants produce seeds and fruits, and many trees lose their leaves. Some animals store food to eat during the cold winter.

A springtime scene in England. The warm spring weather brings out new leaves and flowers.

Forever Changing

Sunshine is hottest at midday when the Sun is highest in the sky. The warm ground heats the air, so afternoons are quite warm too.

As the Sun sets, the land and the air slowly cool down. The coldest time is usually just before dawn. Then, as the Sun rises, the land and the air warm up again.

Children paddle in a pool of rain water on a cool but sunny day in autumn.

Camels and people walk across the Sahara Desert. It is very hot here during the day, but it gets cold at night. There is little rain here.

CLOUDS

The air contains tiny particles of water which are too small to see. Sometimes the particles join together to form clouds of tiny water droplets.

Clouds can make a hot day cooler. When the Sun goes behind a cloud, you feel cooler. But at night, clouds act like a duvet. They stop the land and the air cooling down so quickly.

The Earth as seen from space. In this photo clouds cover the South Pole and swirl over the ocean. Most of the land has clear, sunny weather.

Clouds help us to predict the weather. If these thick clouds become any blacker, they may bring rain. High, wispy clouds mean good weather.

A heavy frost on leaves and fruits glistens in the morning sun.

Mist, Fog and Frost

Mist and fog are clouds which are so low that they touch the ground. Mist and fog form as cold air sinks towards the ground and mixes with warm, moist air trapped beneath it.

Frost is tiny crystals of ice. It is made when water droplets on the ground freeze. Frost usually forms at night, when it is colder, and melts during the day.

A thick mist clings to the mountains in Yosemite National Park, USA.

RAINFALL

Rain comes from clouds. When the droplets in a cloud become too big and heavy to stay in the air, they fall as rain. Rain waters plants and fills puddles, rivers and reservoirs.

Plants, animals and people cannot live without water. But if too much rain falls, the water cannot drain away and sometimes causes a flood.

THE WATER CYCLE

The world's water is always on the move. It falls as rain, goes into rivers, lakes and the sea, and then turns back into cloud.

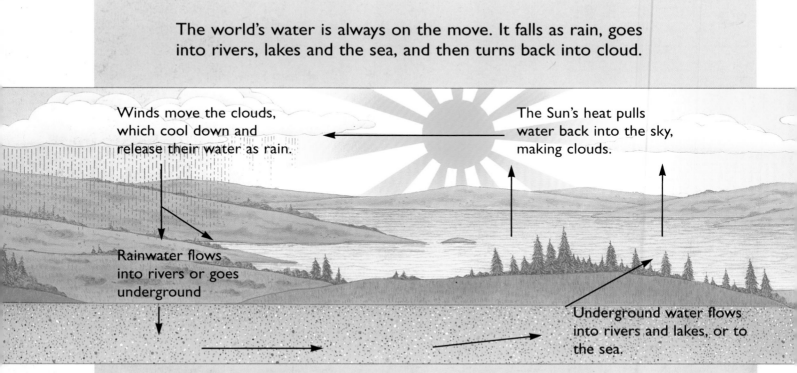

Winds move the clouds, which cool down and release their water as rain.

The Sun's heat pulls water back into the sky, making clouds.

Rainwater flows into rivers or goes underground

Underground water flows into rivers and lakes, or to the sea.

These Japanese boys are
on their way to school.
Their umbrellas will
help to keep them dry
in the rain.

Snow and Hail

Snowflakes are bits of frozen cloud. When water droplets in clouds freeze, they stick together to make flakes of snow. If the ground is freezing, the snow settles.

Hailstones are frozen raindrops. The hailstones get bigger as more ice forms around them. When they are too heavy to stay in the air, they drop to the ground.

Hailstones cover a road in Natal, South Africa. Hailstones batter crops and can even kill animals.

Snow can be fun! These people are skiing in the mountains in France.

WIND

Wind is a mass of moving air. You can feel even a gentle breeze blowing on your skin. Strong winds bend trees and whip up waves on the sea and lakes.

Air can move huge distances, across seas and continents. Winds that blow from warmer countries bring warm air and weather. But winds that blow from the North or South Poles feel especially cold.

A breezy day at Portland Head, Maine, USA. The wind whips up waves which crash against the harbour wall and cliffs.

This man is using the wind to blow his windsurfer across the water near Sydney, in Australia.

FIERCE WEATHER

A tornado in Texas. Tornadoes are called 'twisters' in the USA.

A hurricane is a huge storm that starts over the ocean near the Equator. Hurricanes often move towards land. Strong winds suck up damp air into huge spinning clouds. When the hurricane hits land, it uproots trees and smashes houses.

A tornado always starts on land. It is smaller but fiercer than a hurricane. It spins across the land destroying trees and buildings. Some tornadoes even lift trucks into the air.

These houses and fields have flooded after a hurricane.

Thunder and Lightning

A flash of lightning is a huge, electrical spark in the sky. Lightning heats the air so fast that it explodes in a rumble of thunder. Light travels faster than sound, so you see the flash before you hear the thunder.

Lightning strikes near Perth in Australia.

Lightning is most likely to strike the tallest thing around. Tall buildings have metal lightning conductors to take the electricity safely to the ground.

The sky lights up as a flash of lightning forks through the clouds.

WEATHER FORECASTING

Scientists can forecast, or work out likely changes in the weather. By studying the weather in several places, they create weather maps.

Weather maps show the directions of winds and whether the winds are bringing rain or snow clouds, or hot, dry air.

This white box is called a Stevenson's Screen. It contains special instruments to help scientists record changes in the weather.

Many people rely on weather forecasts. Farmers try to harvest their crops before it rains. Fishermen want to avoid storms at sea. Aircraft pilots need to be warned of fog, lightning and hurricanes.

Meteorologists (scientists who study weather) use powerful computers to help make their forecasts.

WEATHER FACTS AND FIGURES

Hottest place
The hottest temperature ever recorded in the shade was 58° C in Libya in September 1922.

In Wyndham in western Australia it is over 32° C most days in the year.

Coldest place
The coldest temperature ever recorded was just over ⁻89° C, that is 89 degrees below freezing. It was recorded at Vostok in Antarctica in July 1983.

Wettest place
On Mount Wai-'ale-'ale on the island of Kauai in Hawaii it rains on 350 of the 365 days in the year.

Heaviest downpour
In March 1962 rain fell on the island of Réunion in the Indian Ocean to a depth of nearly 2 metres.

Driest place
All deserts are very dry, but the Atacama Desert in Chile is the driest. It gets no rain for years on end.

Strongest wind
The fastest winds are whipped up in storms. In April 1958 a tornado struck Wichita Falls in Texas, USA, with winds of 450 kilometres per hour.

Biggest hailstone
In April 1986 giant hailstones each weighing nearly a kilogramme fell on Bangladesh. They killed 92 people and are the heaviest on record.

Heaviest snowstorm
In just six days in February 1959 nearly 5 metres of snow fell on Mount Shasta Ski Bowl in California.

Speed of lightning
Lightning travels at 140,000 kilometres per second. Sound travels much slower, at about 335 metres per second. To find out how far away a thunderstorm is, count the seconds between the flash of lightning and the rumble of thunder. Divide the number by 3 to get the distance in kilometres.

Further Reading
All Ways of Looking at Weather by J. Walker, (Franklin Watts, 1994).

Living with the Weather series (Wayland, 1997).

The Weather series, all titles by Jillian Purcell (Wayland, 1992).

What Makes it Rain? by Susan Mayes (Usborne, 1995).

Why do we have wind and rain? by Claire Llewellyn (Heinemann, 1995).

The World's Weather by David Flint (Wayland, 1992).

Ice-skating in Manhattan.

GLOSSARY

Breeze A light wind.

Cloud Millions of tiny water droplets floating together in the air.

Crystals Solids with regular, flat sides.

Electricity Energy which can be changed into light, heat, sound or movement.

Fog Low cloud close to the ground.

Forecast To try to work out what is likely to happen.

Lightning conductors Special parts of tall buildings which guide lightning safely down to the ground.

Particles Single, tiny pieces of an object. A particle of water is the smallest amount of water that can exist on its own.

Poles The Earth's furthest points to the north and south. Polar regions have cold temperatures all year round.

Reservoirs Lakes for storing water. Reservoirs are often made by building a dam across a valley to hold back the water in rivers.

Seasons In temperate countries, the year is divided into four main seasons – spring, summer, autumn and winter – according to the usual temperature of the weather. In countries near the Equator, the temperature is mostly the same throughout the year but there are wet and dry seasons. Polar regions are cold all year round.

Temperate A word used to describe the climate of countries that have four seasons.

Temperature A measurement which shows how hot or cold something is.

Thermometer An instrument for measuring temperature.

Wind Moving air.

INDEX